Mosaic

by Joy Horakova

DORRANCE
PUBLISHING CO
EST. 1920
PITTSBURGH, PENNSYLVANIA 15238

Dorrance Publishing Co
585 Alpha Drive
Suite 103
Pittsburgh, PA 15238
Visit our website at www.dorrancebookstore.com

ISBN: 979-8-89211-415-8
eISBN: 979-8-89211-900-9

Stained Glass

Stained...

I feel stained
Red paint across the face
Blue fury spilled in deformations
Yellow lost in an eclipse
Orange sizzling embers
But it's what I was given
I have no choice but to make something out of this

...Glass...

I feel cut
I've seen life pour out of my veins trying to inhabit someone who couldn't
risk a needle for me
I've bled to keep someone's lungs singing
Cut like glass and torched shut
But in the summit of my misery I found my art

But
Put the two together and you have something beautiful
Shards of something once painful and wicked
Pillars of iridescence once shattered now stand
When the light hits, all brokenness is illuminated
And the empty space is filled with redemption

Ashes

Picking yourself up from Jericho's ashes isn't a simple act, it's a slow process
So I blow on the embers and make a fire again

Chambers

You're about to enter the chambers of someone we all know
The culmination of a person we all recognize
The elements of someone we have escaped
The one we talk to a therapist about longer than we want
The one who runs after you just as you realize it's time to run away
The one who comes back just as you're healing
The one you fall the hardest for and rise the strongest without
This is the mosaic chamber of what happened and what's left

Crucible

Someone came into my life looking like a warm fire to sit by
But life around him was a crucible
The high temperatures didn't create anything
They didn't weld together two substances
It didn't shape glass figures or resize white gold
No, it just burned

The burn from this fire didn't shock me this time
Life around him was a crucible
His words sometimes spoke of gentleness
But he was rigid to the slightest touch
Maybe I'm just used to it
But under the numbness it hurts

Pollution

He talks about his life
His dedication to his work
His yearly trips to Coventry
and how he likes to volunteer at church

He mentioned he has a brother
They seem pretty close
Our conversations took a turn
I think he told me things that no one else knows

It all feels so real
So authentic and vaguely deep
We don't need to use many words
It's sickening but so enticing, to put it lightly

I talked about my life
The secret scenes that lay behind
Our time together just seems special
Or maybe it's pollution in my mind

The Difference

He's a one-way street
I'm a four-lane road
He speaks in distance
Yet still motions me close

I'm a mapped out plan
He's a sudden surprise
I should be wary
but oh my oceans, his eyes

I'm a peaceful morning
He's a late-night swoon
I'm a little library
He's a fire-lit room

He keeps me at arms' length
I wear my heart on my sleeve
He has me curious
The way he beckons for me

The collision can clash
I may not understand
But sometimes the stains
End up going hand in hand

Thin Ice

He found me on the frozen water gliding on a thin blade
He'd spin around then fall
It sent a rose tint to my face

I pull my fingers down into the center of my glove
I'm shivering but I'm hiding it
I want to see what this hour does

He took my arms and pulled me in twice
Both rhythmic and feeble
It feels like carving hearts but on thin ice

Phantom

Each time we embrace I can't seem to forget
Every time you brush my arm it lingers on my skin
You're like a breeze or a phantom limb

My body remembers your heat to its core
But being gaze locked with you feels like stone
Would I be okay just laying with your ghost?

I'm lost in your mystery just so you know
Your secrecy whispers the gentlest anthem
I could be yours...
...But you end up a phantom

Metallica T-shirt

I thought of you the entire time
I slept in a Metallica T-shirt that wasn't mine
I was restless so he poured me wine
The entire night felt like a crime

He made the dark feel somehow bright
He brought the fireworks for my July
I still found traces of you in his eyes
While in a Metallica T-shirt that wasn't mine

Something about his gaze didn't feel right
I knew I was walking a dangerous line
I calculated the consequences once or twice
But I thought of breaking rules with you in candlelight

Touch

There's something like a magnetic force when two physical touch love languages collide. You touch me as if to absorb every second of it that I give you. It's like my skin becomes brail and you're reading every word it tells you. It wants you as close at possible.

Shift

So I try to shift my thoughts to a new space
Not to cologne, the music, or the art that hangs on either side of your fireplace
I try to reign in the emotion but out it slips
If poetry had a taste it'd be found at your dangerous lips

When a Boy Fancies a Bookworm

He asks me what books I'm currently reading, and I don't think any other gentleman has ever been so thoughtful

May

You ask to see me on your birthday
It was the brightest day we ever had in May

You ask me to lay next to you
It was as close to happy tears I'd felt in years

Your arms motioned for me
It was the most dangerous place I'd ever laid

All the sirens were going off
It was the loudest sound I'd ever drowned out

A Trick

I tricked myself into thinking that a kiss is just a kiss
We all know that's never the case. At least not for me

I tricked myself into thinking that a minute won't matter
We all know minutes turn to hours. At least for us

I tricked myself into thinking this means something for us
We all know that's not how it ends. At least not for you

The Influence of Enchantment

I'm going to over think things
I'm going to run these gears to their very end
Because you're telling me to trust you
To give into the influence of enchantment

I'm going to put my thoughts to rest
Because I know you'll be gentle
And you know I'll be honest
Under your influence of enchantment

When Something Feels Off

I'm a bit off my axis
Where my thoughts are restless
and my heart is torn
Suddenly breathing
is all deepening
to synchronize yours

That thing in your orbit
comes spinning toward me
but never on time
Suddenly conviction
arises suspicions
in my clouded mind

I'm reminiscing
It took some convincing
yet I implore
You never end up with
ever the one
you fall the hardest for

Persuasion

I don't think I should ever be alone with you again
But oh my oceans, that's the only place I want to be right now

I don't think I should risk another step, another text
But oh my oceans, his persuasion is as smooth as satin

Lust

Somewhere between all the late nights, secrets, a warm hand to hold,
The firelight, our four eyes, and the craziest lies I've ever told,
I fell in lust
And I admit it now in hindsight

～∪∪～

Tangled

But how will I ever choose
Between desire and a future with no proof
That's the web I'm tangled in when it comes to you

But how will I ever choose
When poison can taste like nectar too
That's the web I'm tangled in when it comes to you

But someone tell me how
This far this fast is something I allowed
I'm thinking "Poison" will be your new name now

Parallels

The thing is, we're two parallels, we were never meant to intersect and meet the way we want to, and the more you force it, the harder the lines break. That's why I can't see you again.

Poison

I observe for a while
Kept my safe distance
Not allowing another step
Rehearsing all my lines
Building up courage I thought I lacked
But then you message me
I stare at the poison...and tip it back

Illusions

Be careful around optical Illusions
They were created to draw you in
They are styled to captivate
They're authored to allure
Are you sitting, standing, moving, falling hard, or lying perfectly still?

As enticing as they are, their nature is to trick you
That's simply their makeup

...Don't let him

Question

Don't leave me living in question
Making up my own ending
Or pretending I already know
Every answer unspoken

Don't ask for my moments
While you know I'm alone
Only to keep me on a misguided rope
Tell me or let me go

If it's not going to be you then
Quit blocking my view
Look at my heart and see there's no room
It's time to make you move

Parasite

We're lost in an echo
Getting oddly intertwined
The igniting essence of Calvin Klein

Every second absorbed
Not yet wanting to go home
But you only reach for me when we're alone

My buttons are fragile
and you keep on pressing
I believed you cared, but now I'm second guessing

I live in the simple
You bask in all the finer
You tell me eloquent tales in the key of E Minor

The way you speak
You innocence claim
It was all a script in your twisted play

I'm going to run until I forget your name

Perennials

In hues of rainbow you'd visit each spring and summer then disappear
when it got cold
Your sunny magnitude would draw me back each time but my does it get old

You can't come and go as you please like spring flowers in each trip
around the sun
I don't know what exactly I am to you but to me you're not just anyone

You show up in wild whispers and the sweetest touch, I never knew what
to do
So I stare for a moment and contemplate, then pull you from the root

Red Handed

You were a mystery
A question of heart
You spoke to me softly
So I let down my guard

You told me to trust you
I thought you were safe
But suddenly I look down
I'm covered in red paint

Your smile was a trick
Your hands behind your back
When I get a second look
You had the paint on your hands

Stained Memories

Maybe it didn't feel right
Perhaps I overshared
All I know is I saw you one night
And it all went downhill from there

I should have been more cautious
Everything you said sounded true
You led me on for months
And kept me envisioning you

Twirling out of orbit
Heading straight into the ground
A dizzy drop of stardust
Exploding on its way down

It's Fine, I'm Fine

I lie to the face of all of my friends
The worst part is I don't know that I'm lying yet
You made me a liar
Apathy's best friend
It's fine, I'm fine
I convince myself lying awake at 2 a.m.

Person

Personality doesn't justify mistreatment
Perseverance doesn't equal victory
Performance without an audience
Perplexed in your sharp artistry
Persuasion is always exposed
You've personified deception

The Thing with You

I wanna go with you
I wanna talk Taylor Swift with you
I wanna just drift with you
I don't want anyone to know that I still haven't quit you
That I still give a shit about you
And that's the thing
That's the thing with you

I just don't get you
It makes no sense that I miss you
That I still wanna kiss you
So I deny and deny but I know that's the shit truth
I hesitate but
That's the thing
That's the thing with you

All I Know

I don't know if you took more than I wanted to give
Or if I gave more than you wanted to take
All I know is that there's an indent on my arms where you once held me
and whispered my name

I don't know if I had what you wanted
or if I was something that you already had
All I know is you just disappeared, and I thought I at least meant more to
you than that

Heart

I don't know what it was that you thought I wanted, and I have fears about that...But I wanted absolutely nothing from you. Nothing except your heart

Convincing Myself of Made-up Tales

He'd be hollow
I'm sure he'd forget to call
or show up hours later and act like he didn't know
and if I convince myself of that
Maybe I'll stop looking back

He wouldn't talk
I'm sure he'd close up
and act like I'm the once who's wrong
If I convince myself of this
Maybe I won't miss him

He'd be distant
I'm sure I'd be lonely
If we'd go out I'm sure he wouldn't listen
If I convince myself of this
I'll stop lingering

It was all in my head
My own exaggerations
He never meant the things he said
If I convince myself of that
I'll never risk such a thing again

Disposable

To make a person disposable
I've learned what that feels like several times now

⌇⌇⌇

New Year's Eve

Trying not to self-destruct full throttle
Trying not to drink the whole damn bottle
But it's New Year's Eve
And I just thought you'd think of me
But now I'm—

Dressed up like a midnight Barbie
Stuck going stag to a party
I'm not lonely but I'm alone
That might sink in on the drive home

It's not like me to do this
It was his own flaws yet I feel foolish
Cause it's New Year's Eve
And I read in to you texting me
But now I'm—

Dressed up with Dior perfume
Only unkissed dame in a full room
I'm not lonely but I'm alone
And my heart just might turn into stone

I want to toughen and say he missed out
But if he called I'd crumble all the way down
Still it's New Year's Eve
And I want to make the most for me
So now I'm—

Dressed up like a midnight Barbie
Laughing at a cocktail party
I'm sitting ready counting down
Resolving for a better year with better choices now

What You Should Have Said

"Hey, I'm sorry but I don't see a future with us
I've tried and don't have it in me anymore
Thank you for understanding; I wish you well, of course"

You really shouldn't have to say much
But it shouldn't have kept me guessing
It would have put an end to all these feelings I've been wrestling

What You Could Have Said

"Truly, I never really saw us being together
You're too much and were just a void fill in my life
You're not even my type, but a way to pass the time"

You could have just been honest
You could have run me over with your words
Instead you just said nothing, which is a different kind of hurt

What I Would Have Said Back

"Wow, I do admire your honesty
I know that sounds like a straight-out lie
But now that I finally know, I can move on with my life"

Thank you, my precious Poison
For your time and for a piece of your small heart
You taught me how to read the signs and to not let down my guard

Fiction

If only I could make him into fiction
I'd really only reverse the endings—

I'd let her meet him
I'd let him sound enticing
But I'd write her in a conscious
I'd keep *him* dreaming nightly

I'd let him keep talking
Of his travels and daily splendor
But she'd get bored and doze off gently
And go off to find someone better

They'd go months without a word
Yet he'd want her as a lover
But one day she'd stop responding
And *he'd* have to live in constant wonder

If only I could make him into fiction
I'd change my fate unknowingly
If only I could make him into fiction but I can't
So I pound out the words in poetry

Mix Tape

If I had to make it into a mixed tape

It would start with a little "Dear John" by Taylor Swift
It'd be "I Will Let You Go" by Daniel Ahearn but just starting at the key change of the bridge

It'd be "Hiding My Heart" by Adele being sung on the way home
The words would definitely be "Edge of Desire" by John Mayer while at sitting all alone

It'd be all the words of "Gravity" by Sarah Barellis echoing in the hall
Then end with "Memory I Don't Mess With" by Lee Brice and that would say it all

In A Few Years' Time

I feel like in a few years' time I'm going to look back with an aerial view
And regret the touch, the thought or even the glimpse of you

In a few years' time I'm going to count how many times you took another shot
And remember that forgiving is a strength but forgetting is not

In a few years' time I'm going to have ALL that I've been chasing
And you might upgrade your house to fill the elsewhere spacing

As a Defense

In this last time face to face I teeter on the edge of being rude
And I think you know it's a facade because I can't risk an inch turning
into the mile that I know I'm prone to
And what you can't see is that this anger is a mask because I don't hate
you, I just care so damn much and have no reason for that because it's
clear that element was not reciprocated

Deep Down I Know It

Sometimes I wish I could hate you, or even simply dislike you but I can't. Because despite what happened and didn't happen, I still believe it was not your intent to hurt me.

When Habits Turn into Lifestyles

I feel like you'll always try to see how far over the line you can push me to But then make it a habit and end up pushing away the one that was actually meant for you. Maybe you already have

Best Wishes

I don't wish ill on you
I don't wish I never met you
I just wish you'd change
Be better for whoever comes next

I don't wish you hell
I don't wish you heartbreak
I just wish you'd learn
Be kinder for the wiser of womanhood

I don't wish you hardship
I don't wish you sleeplessness
I just wish you'd grow
Be better, by God, be better for whoever comes next

Unlucky Stars

Dear unlucky stars, what's going on?
I don't know what to say, it's like I'm playing Scrabble with my tongue

Dear unlucky stars, look at where we are
How on earth did I let him walk up and play a pendulum with my heart?

Dear unlucky stars, I wish I may, I wish I might
Maybe I just enjoyed what being fancied by him felt like

Dear unlucky stars, nothing happened, so why is it so hard?
Why do I still feel the shiver from his touch running down my arm?

Collateral Damage

So I guess I dodged a bullet,
So why do I still feel like I'm getting hit?

Simple

As much as I like putting my emotions in the simplest of terms
this ended up being an era that was matchless to words

That says a lot about you
and a lot about me in response to you

I Deserve Better Part One

He told me he's limitless, but I deserve better

He told me he's gentle, but I deserve better

He told me he's important, but I deserve better

It's not that I think I'm owed the world, but I deserve better than to sec-
ond guess who I am to someone

Therapy

I tried to catch the clouds
I tried to catch a break

I can't make it something to grasp
I can't make it a punching bag

I tried to sing it like a Taylor Swift song
I tried to ignore the chest pang

I can't trick myself into being okay
I can't get away with anything these days

I tried to write about it to work it out
I tried but failed so I talk to a therapist now

What's The Game? Part One

Hey Miss Therapist,
I'm not sure how to describe how I feel so bear with me as I try—

I don't know what I feel, Miss Therapist,
But if the game is baseball
My heart was the ball and took a hit
And he ran the bases as I went flying

I don't know how to play, Miss Therapist,
It's like the game is poker
I live life bluffing the whole way through it
And I always fear being found out

I don't know what to do, Miss Therapist,
But if the game is hide and seek
I'm the one hiding and can't take it
I thought I'd be the one seeking

Therapy Part Two

What is it about me that makes me such an easy target for this level of
sharpened manipulation? This suave stab. This poisonous person.
Tell me, Miss Therapist. Is it me or was it him?
If you could visualize my emotions, they would be blue, dark and dim

Abstract

Viewpoints

Look at the mosaic from a different angle
See it from a topical height
Yes, you might have to climb a little
But the abstract will shine in different light

Visualize the design on a different wall
We often lose sight in the midst of pain
But if you just step back you'll realize that
Maybe to lose love is hard but to see anew is gain

Why

Why is the biggest abstract question you could ever ask
It's almost a black hole that could never render its motive or resolve
Instead of breathing in its circulating anonymity
Exhale the distrust with shooting back at the word itself—
"Why not?"

Art Fragments

So the glass is stained
The dust has settled
The diamonds turned back to coal
I lost a few buttons
I stand in Jericho's ashes
Right here I find that I have every particle I need

Recovery

People subconsciously go looking for what's missing in their lives and often fall victim to the low standards they've always known. They simply settle for what's familiar, what fills the gaps and not necessarily what's best. I am Joy, and I am in recovery from this

Healing

I'm not looking for a distraction
I'm not looking for a person
I'm not even looking for companionship
I'm looking for myself on the other side of healing
And there's no set timeline for that

Swing Low

Swing low, my hopes and dreams
Come for me
Let me latch on to your untethered strings
Swing me faster until I let go
Watch me fly
And land somewhere in the middle
Trying to find the height I once knew
So swing low

Due Recognition

I recognize it's my choice to sit in my own offense
And it's not my job to make anyone see things through my lens

I also recognize it's my choice to see the best in me
And the grass is greener wherever I confidently stomp my feet

The Right Combination

Everything will be fine, just give it sleep, espresso, and time

Trusting No One

I prefer allowing myself to feel rather than play dead
But I'm sick of staring at mascara stains on my bedspread

I understand the circumstances but still feel timid
Searching every heart and each one seems more wicked

I tell myself I'm strong enough to take on the seasons
But that doesn't mean I like it and you've read all my reasons

Me

I learn about myself every day
Who I really am
I have a soft heart
And learned how someone could take advantage of that

I'm still growing as a person
That's how I am
I have a strong backbone
And how dare anyone think it should come under attack

I'm learning to love me again
Just the way I am
I have a guard up still
But every time I fall, I rise with an even bigger comeback

Authenticity

A soft heart,
A strong backbone
A kind smile
Thick skin

People who test your authenticity are only battling with their own

I Deserve Better Part Two

The truth is I don't have one brush of my skin available for anyone claiming their innocence in dimly lit rooms. My standards are a mile high now.

Realizing Who I Am

I don't know when I started distrusting myself
If you grasp too hard, I could hurt you with my spears
If you're not careful you might draw blood
I lose pieces of myself as time goes on, and I don't fully understand that concept
I'm soft, delicate, but I long to be strong
I'm red in the face, gray along my edges
When I'm dry I crumble...

I don't know why I didn't see my true self
But I'm a signature of romance
I'm a symbol of one's heart
I have a thirsty soul and a blooming spirit
I'm a marvelous gift of thought and fancy
I brighten rooms with an aroma of beauty
Oh yeah, I'm a rose

Who Will Be the One Part One

Okay, will anyone ever be gentle with me?
Can anyone speak to me softly?
Does anyone have any kindness?
I'm longing and lost for any shred of tenderness, compassion
Will anyone be gentle with me?

Anyone? Bueller?

I went out to walk around
I'm picking up pieces of my trust all over town
Wanting someone's time
While they seem to only want my moments
It's like everyone's playing games
Is there anyone out there who's truly honest?

Capable of Love Part One

Sometimes I wish I wasn't capable of love
So I wouldn't know the pain of loss
The desolate nights of isolation
The games and unreturned texts
The absence of a dog readjusting in the middle of the night
The impact of losing a grandparent
Sometimes, I wish I wasn't capable of love

When I Met the One Who Mattered

I was getting so fed up
At the end of my emotional rope
Thinking that nobody is honest
And my love has no place to go

Life revolved around working
And just trying hard to make it by
I had come to expect nothing
Until you came around and said hi

Two spoons over dessert
I found I'm leaning in close
Your words flowed like poetry
Or like some song I wanted to know

I find myself being a tad shy
Cause in a past life I've been shattered
But my guard was crumbling down
When I met the one who mattered

Slow

Take it slow
Just take me somewhere...anywhere
Anywhere with you

Finally

It was a kiss that tasted like finally
It was a collision that made a clash
It was an embrace that felt like home
It was a kiss that tasted like finally

Third Date

Getting ready for the third date
He's picking me up from my house
My happy hormones pump with a heavy pulse

The Drunk Girl

She was over served
And pulled at your clothes
You could have
And no one would have known

You took her upstairs
Lay her on the bed
Made sure she was safe
And then you just left

It could have been trauma
But you knew how to act
I guess I'm just saying
Thank you for that

I fell in love a little
As this story sunk in
This is how it feels to
Know I'm safe again

Safe

A few weeks in and it's going well
He has the safest arms I've ever felt

~⌣⌣~

Flame

I never thought I'd be able to relate to someone that way again
There was a dwindling flame inside me, and he offered the soft wisp of his
breath on the embers

Red Room

Come into my red room
Bring the black prints
Dissipate in honesty
See what becomes of it

I'm going to warn you
This will take time
To illuminate the picture
At the scene of the crime

I Could Feel My Heart Smiling

Oh the day when I caught you smelling my hair.
The look on your face is forever burned in my brain

Silhouette

I didn't think it would be possible
How could I ever let
Anyone ever get this close again?
So I'll hesitate and then
Allow myself to finally forget
And fall into his silhouette

Who Will Be the One Part Two

I lamented to heaven with dreams of delicacy
Desires of comfort and the slightest courtesy
Who will be gentle and who will understand?
He stood up firmly and said, "I'll be the man"

I second guess cause my trust tank is low
If I ever saw pure honesty, would I even know?
I've been hiding behind my own walls for so long
When I say, "Who will climb?" he said, "I'll be the one!"

Tell Me

Tell me who you are
Tell me who you'll be
Look inside my heart
Stare into my eyes
I guess what I'm saying is
Tell me
Tell me what it would be like

I'll Be Patient

"You can tell me what you think I need to know when you're ready. No rush, Joy."

I twist and turn in awkward conversation
I stammer and stumble
Let my heart fall on the pavement

But you whisper softly to me,
"I'll be the one who's patient"

Shalom

If anyone wreaking of poison asked to see me again, I'd get to say no because nothing is missing from my life anymore and that's an immeasurable power. It's shalom—nothing missing, nothing broken.

Maybe I'll Say It

Maybe I'm afraid to say it too soon
So I say it to the sky, the stars, and the moon
Maybe one day you'll find me admitting
Maybe one day we'll get the ending we wanted from the beginning

Oh My Oceans

A kaleidoscope of pacific blues
Your gravity pulls me into you
I didn't know what a simple glance could do
You have me locked up in an abstract view
Like hurricane waves crashing into you

Smiling

How do I hold in this smile?
How do I contain this joy?
So on a park bench
With the book that you sent
I'm reading all the signs again

Melt Me

I'm awkward but comfortable
But perfectly myself when it's just us
We give each other freedom
You say I make awkward look gorgeous

Stability

I thought I knew what to expect
Fun, excitement, a few bickers,
but I never knew to expect stability
I guess I've never known what that's like

Thinking in Terms

Thinking in terms of writing home
Of telling Mom that she'll like this one

Thinking in terms of tomorrow
And not making me wait another day

Thinking in terms of the long haul
Knowing he's someone my family will love

Meeting the Family

Chances are my Mom will love you
Though she might come off as a little reserved
She's just been hurt and now is skeptical
And trust me that's really not like her

Chances are my brother will love you
I can see the two of you getting along
You'll both make jokes and laugh it off
I can't think of anything more I'd want

Chances are my friends will listen more than talk
They may say erratic things simply just to test you
They've seen me hurt and help me rebuild
And when my heart breaks so does theirs now too

Rest Easy

They'll ask about your job,
The back-up plan you got
And I just know that you'll impress them

It might take a time or two
Of me overly defending you
But finally I'm prepared for every question

What I Like About You

You reach for me while brushing hands
You've never once denied me a dance

You're someone my brother finally likes
You never let the sun go down on a fight

You listened as I explain the depths of my heart
Understand when I said dreaming for me is still hard

You said, "Well, Love, make it into art"

Stay With Me

I want to get the words out but I can't
so I say them with my eyes
I think I'm asking you to stay the night

If you stay we can chat or not chat
You tell me with your warmth
You're okay with all of that

No Words, Just Rest

Just come and meet me
Where thoughts can flow freely
And words are obsolete

Home with You

I like sleeping diagonally across the bed,
Blasting Taylor Swift at 8 a.m.

I like buying decorative pink pillows,
On cold autumn days opening up all the windows

I like white sheets and pitch-black nights,
warm blankets and the fan on high

But if none of this works

I'll try my best to stay to my side
I'll wake up late with you on my mind

If you don't like the color, we can switch to green
Only crack the windows once or twice a week

I'll change it all like this is your home too
As long as every day I come home to you

If It Didn't Work Out

At this point I think my Mom would cry
She would take me for a drive
She'd want to know but would be afraid to ask

Dad would ask what's been happenin'
I burry my head in his arms and then
Feel his arms tighten around me with a tear

My friends would take me out for wine
They'd listen and maybe stay the night
Because they'd see through my every fake act

I don't want to weigh the odds
While out here getting lost in thought
I know there's no one else that could be for me

And That's How I Know

I know where my heart is because my mind always wanders back to you
I know where you stand because you've never stepped outside of anchored
I know where we are because you've never let there be room for doubt

Yours, Mine, & Ours

Your thoughts
My words
Our actions
Their judgments
Your heart
My hands
Our collision
Their loss

What's The Game? Part Two

Hey Therapist,
I have so much to tell you and am not sure how so please bear with me as I try

I don't know where to start, Miss Therapist
But if the game was baseball
I held the bat, took a swing, and made the hit
I was in control this time around

I'm not sure how it happened, Miss Therapist
But if the game was poker
I thought the hand I was dealt was a trick
Regardless I figured it out and won

One more thing, Miss Therapist
If the game was hide-and-seek
I sought and sought and now I see it
And I made it into something new

Collage

Composition

A unique montage of disconnected worlds
A piecing of uneven particles
A collage of puzzles and pictures
But together, stand back, observe, it all makes sense

Something I Haven't Felt in a While

His steps and my stumbles
He leads and I trip
I fall and he catches
We're awkward but we're trying
Dancing with him feels like flying

Willful Intent

Yes, it's a mess
My past and your present
But it just doesn't matter
I'll give you my best
The good and the bad
I'll take every bit
We'll unravel and forget all the rest

I promise you my willful intent
In the measure of heart
And the words to the breaths
But words never mean all that they're meant

Inspiration

I've outgrown memories
I've moved passed flashbacks
It's time to use these elements as inspiration
A reflection of what I'll never have to endure again

The Craving of a Cold Day

I just want to come home, collapse on your shoulder and say this day has
been rough,
unwind in your eyes, and relax in your hug
I just want to come home, curl up on the couch, and lay on your chest
The craving of a cold day is just to sync to your breath

Find Someone

Find someone who will be patient as you mend
Find someone who will listen as you process
Find someone who will work with your frailty
Find someone who sees your hidden strength
Then decide to love that someone
Love that someone with all you have

Be The One

Be the one who's patient as they grow
Be the one who listens as they vent
Be the one who strives through weakness
Be the one who sees the underlying power
Even if it's just for yourself
Be the one who does good

Blend

We can call the past blue
We can call the present red
We can keep everything separate
Or make the perfect blend

Bring me your colors
Let's make something great
It doesn't have to make sense
Just pour out the paint

Falling

I'm falling in excitement
I'm falling in fun
It's not enough to say that
I'm falling in love

I'm falling in gently
I'm falling down slow
I'm falling in a movement
That I've never known

I'm falling in joy
I'm falling in deep
I'm falling hard
But I'm falling safely

Love vs. Time

I don't believe in measuring love against time
You could live a lifetime with someone and be numb
You could just meet someone and instantly know what they'll mean to you

New Seasons

In the perspective of seasons, he feels like the first day of spring
The sensation of warmth in April
Color-bursting view at the top of the hill
A hot drink in the first snowfall
A kiss every New Year's Eve
He feels like rose pedals on February 14th
Like a collage of excitement everyday

The Senses

If he were a texture he'd be velvet
If he were a sound he'd be soft lake waves
If he were a color he'd be navy
If he were a taste he'd be cinnamon
If he were a scent he'd be home
The simplest, the well known, the best

Dream Catcher

You spun webs for me to fall into
They were thick and strong
Like they'd carry my bodyweight
Like nothing would fall through the weaves
I was never used to being caught

You spun these webs intentionally
They are mighty and metaphoric
What are they there for?
But they weren't meant for my body
They were meant for the fullness,
The every element of my dreams

You spun these webs for me
The dreams that have once fallen
The ones I thought were dead
You wanted to catch every single one
So now I think of you every time I see
Your dream catcher hanging over my bed

Four-Word Testimonies

I kept on going
I chose to work
I chose to win
I laughed at naysayers
Some losses were necessary
I burned some bridges
I made many changes
I got over myself
I accepted good counsel
I set an example
I didn't give up

The Irrelevant

What happened in the past I don't even remember
those memories flew away like dust on the slamming shutters

Walking Beside

He's walked with me through snow and sun
I tell him everything and he keeps his composure
He painted so brightly all of my Octobers

You Hear What I Don't Say

I've spent my last few years going so unheard
Why is it, with you, I don't even need words?

I've spent too long suppressing my thoughts
Why is it that you can somehow hear them all?

Shocking Comparisons

I hate that I'm surprised by being treated right
I hate that I'm shocked by gentleness
But at the same time, I love you for being the one to show me

Just Say It

I don't want to speak in metaphors of season, music, or mosaics in shades of blue, I just want to tell you boldly that I'm falling in love with you

Echo

My words dance like raindrops on the water
Like paint running down a canvas
Like a peaceful chill in a spring breeze

My words whisper like an artist's inspiration
It's like a silent echo through the chest
But all I want to do is shout from the mountains that I'm fiercely in love
with you

Suede

In the suede of the couch I drew I heart
In the suede of the couch you drew a "u"
In the suede of the couch I drew an "I" before the heart
Then you said it

One, Two, Three

One life, two hearts, three words
Four hours go by and it's all a blur

White snow, gray eyes, sunrise
Waking up to your hand in mine

With one life, two hearts, three words
It's all on our terms

Simply Because You're Mine

If I lose with everyone else around me
I win every day with you

Perfect Sense

I used to hold on to things and now I just hold on to you and the good
Lord above,
I've never known a state if being like this so that's why I call it love

The Combination of You and I

You can look at me, and my mind feels bound to you
My senses fall defenseless
My guard disintegrates like ash
I can sit in silence with you and be understood
Your sun shines through my stained glass

Canvas

Paint me a better picture
Draw on my back
Draw me in close
Whatever your art, make my body the canvas

Nightmares

"Come on, it's just a kiss," Poison said as he leaned in.

Sweating, panting, I wake up
It was just a dream
It was just a dream

I look over and remember who's next to me
My dreamcatcher

This one we can let fall through
I've let go of that and now sleep peacefully next to you

Forever

At this point I'm not sure what I'd do
If at the end it wasn't you

At that stage or in a different life
I'd look for you in a stranger's eye

Correction

"I miss you" is too light
Searching doesn't measure up
Longing is in the playing field

It's not that I miss you, it's that you're missing from me

Capable of Love Part Two

I'm glad I'm capable of love
The warmth of waking up next to him
The spark of energy pulsating as I pursue greatness
The anticipation of glory in the afterlife

Hell

I think some of my finest art came from walking through fire
I think my best work embarked with the smell of ash on my skin
I think the tallest I've stood was amid the mountains I thought I'd never
conquer
I think the most beautiful places I've ended up was through drifting on
cold waters
In fact, I know that my proudest moments came from walking through hell

Heaven

When I'm asked if I'd do it all over again knowing it brought me here, would I? The answer will always be no. I would never relive the pain. I'll never understand why I had to go through hell to get to heaven.
I'm only glad that I made it and I'm standing.

Taste of Truth

Lies taste great but when you finally taste truth there will be no going back
You'll be starved for honesty for life
That's what you've done for me, that's what I want to do for you

Museum

Exhibit

So he walks with me through each room. Observing the artifacts of the
past, the present, and the dream of the future.
We come upon an exhibit, and I, his tour guide, explain it's fragments—
The origin, how it got here, how it was crafted, why it's featured
He hears my life stories, landmarks, and scars
It's like he fully understands and listens with his heart

Synergy

Come after me
Reach for my hand in distances
Search for me in the galleries
Be my words in writers block
Let's be an audacious synergy

Erosion

Our love is like a soft erosion of sandstone
The unnecessary slips away and leaves behind sculptures of the effect

What Your Love Feels Like

Your love feels like land on the horizon
like coming home, like Saturdays
Like soaring above the clouds at thirty thousand feet
That's what your love feels like to me

Your love feels like a warm embrace
the softest touch, a forehead kiss
Like after years of endless chaos finally knowing safety
That's what your love feels like to me

Your love feels like a picket fence,
a welcome mat, a monogram mailbox
Like morning coffee on the porch on a quiet street
That's what your love feels like to me

Your love feels like creative dates,
garden walks, sunset skyline views in the city
Like priceless paintings just waiting to be seen
That's what your love feel to me

Normal

I don't ever want to go back to normal if normal was what I knew before you.
I don't ever want to go back to familiar if it sacrifices the unknown with you

Timing

If it was any other time or
At any other place in life
I don't think I'd be ready
Or strong enough to fight

Maybe it had to happen
A broken heart or two
To find that my heart
Was out searching for you

Fearless

I used to fear the winter
I once avoided dusty streets
Now I dance in them boldly
As he's holding onto me

I used to hate the shiver
And the outbreak of the cold
But he taught me to be a dreamer
Embracing the new, laughing at the old

There's one more thing
Something I've never felt before
You make the coldest seasons
Somehow gleam with a brand-new warmth

~⌇~

But When I'm With You

I'm strong
I'm a warrior
I can do it all on my own
I don't need anyone's help
...
But when I'm in his arms
I completely disintegrate
I cave when I'm held in your grip
You cultivate ideas of unity
And never any other way

A Life of Unity

In bookstores he walks with me
Sharing coffee cups he listens
In church he stands beside
I stop and reflect, not a dream, but real life

What You Said

"It's not that there was a moment that I felt 'this is it,' it's that there was never a moment where I felt 'this isn't.'"

Four Words

You took me up to the best view
You took my hand
You took my heart
You took my breath
You took a knee
You said four words

Eyes

Open your eyes to see the moment
Close your eyes to feel it
Open your eyes to see him down on one knee
Close your eyes to say yes

Yes

"Yes"
The most beautiful, singular word in poetry.
And I said it to you

You

Forever the love of my life
The forefront of my heart
The background on my phone

〜〜

Wife

He looked at me and said he saw "wife"
I looked at him and said I saw "safety"
My heart is safe
My heart is finally safe
Deep breath
Safe

Tiffany Blue

Something old
Something new
Something borrowed
And Tiffany Blue
I walk the aisle confidently to you

Something tangled
Something torn
Something pretty
And a heart that's yours
I feel these vows down to the core

Something dark
Something bright
Something gray
Something right
and a Tiffany Blue skyline

Love is patient; love is kind...

He has been patient as I navigate falling in love and being loved
He has been so kind to me from the simple act of buying me coffee to the
immeasurable act of teaching me to dream again
He has sought to put others first
He's a warrior of defense and has the warmest heart I've ever known
He is an example of perseverance

Love Does Not Envy

So to you, with all the strength I have,
I am going to try to be patient
I am going to be kind and not envy anything accept your metabolism
I am going to fail at not being boastful because you are everything to brag about
I will honor you as my husband and best friend
We will seek truth, hope, and justice
And because we choose to live in love, we will not fail

March 27th, 2020

Love was in the air
The sun was in the sky
Caffeine was in my system
Our hearts were so close
The chairs were six feet apart

A Wedding Band

You've given me all I've never had
The first being peace of mind
The second, a wedding band

Quarantine

He's my husband
My best friend
My dance partner forever
My quarantine dream

Simple, Beautiful

Books cover the dining room table
Early mornings make me feel old
We're reading quietly to ourselves
As the coffee is getting cold

The unmade bed is lying still
The background noise is the heat on high
It's a simple Saturday snowing hard
But when I zone out, I catch your eye

The calendar is open, it's beautiful
Having no plans to run off to
Just a couple of books and a fireplace
Being perfectly comfortable just being in the same room

Masking

Out of a mask he gave me a masquerade
Out of a party of passers you were the one who stayed
I look at a future with you, and I'm no longer afraid
There's no disguise with you, no paint on your face
Out of nothing look now at the spectacle we've made

Now

Now I look at you with sleepy eyes across my pillowcase
Now I rush home at five just to see your face
Now we drink our coffees and plan weekends at the lake
Where there have been gaps your hands fill the space

It Means Everything

In lieu of all the world has dealt us, it means everything to know the safest place is home with you
In lieu of all the chaos all around, it means everything to get to call anywhere with you my paradise

Our Love

Authors write about this kind of love
Poets search for these kinds of words
Couples try to create these kinds of moments
The world needs more of these stories
and it's ours

Masterpiece

A little piece of broken glass
A couple of pins
A stitch or two
A pear-shaped pin
A few music notes
A maple leaf
A diamond
You, me
We make a mosaic masterpiece

The Art of Dreaming

I get to teach myself how to dream again
I get to look forward and be hopeful
I can experience the joy of wonder
The mystery of discovering

Rare

Find someone who acknowledges that a love like yours is rare

The Great Refocus

I've found that I don't like songs about loss because I feel I've done nothing but gain

I don't like comparisons of defeat because I know that all I've done is win

I don't like thoughts of demolition because all I've done is build

I don't like ideas of ruin because all I've done is restore

Writing

I searched for my feelings in the words of other poets
I listened to the songs of brilliant lyricists
I explored the paintings of travelled artists
I read the love stories of experienced authors
I couldn't find my emotions in the least of these
So I was forced to start creating on my own

Pottery

So I took the clay and molded it into the life I wanted to live.
Even the pieces I thought were no good became something I held in my hands and used to re-create
The edges were rough so I softened them out
and the cracks became light holes where the sun could shine through
My life is a pottery, and I held each particle this whole time

The Head vs. the Heart

My head writes to tell a story
My heart writes to feel the story

My head remembers things chronologically
My heart remembers veins pulsating in the words

My head wants the reader know
My heart wants the reader to understand

My head wants to reader to read
My heart wants the reader to write for themselves so others feel less alone

Observations

Take heed of my mistakes so you don't need to make the same ones
Look at the scraps that have come together while I thought they were fall-
ing a part
Look what I made of shards that once cut me
Stand in the middle and watch the light shine through the broken pieces
Watch it illuminate the daunting darkness
It's not something, it's everything, if that's what you choose

My Museum

Walk through my museum
Each room of trial, whimsy, and odd formations
Learn from each component
Notice each piece
Observe from different perspectives
Walk through my museum
But don't stay there
Just walk through and learn

Late

I'm on time despite the traffic
I'm on time despite the snow
I'm on time for the things I hate
I didn't try, I'm on time although
Now I'm late
In the biggest way
We've brought love and art in to an overflow

Sonogram

I'm a little nervous but I know how this goes
Just relax, take a breath, they tell you what to do
But no one prepares you for the heartbeat
Or when they tell you there's two

Mosaic

You put a diamond on my hand and a melody back into my heart
After being wounded so deeply I said I'd never revisit the art

I'm more than words again, I'm myself, and you're the better half of me
Together we fit and make some kind of roaring symphony

It's pieces of the broken, welded, placed into something new
I think that was the goal, to make a glistening mosaic out of pieces of me
and pieces of you

Thank You

To Patrick, the life of my love, my page 83 and my best friend who shattered every glass ceiling of expectations. I meant what I said in my vows, you are everything to brag about! Thank you for cheering on my every dream, I hope to do the same for you for the rest of our lives.

To Katerina, thank you for believing in this. I don't know if I would have submitted it if not for you. Keep adventuring on my beautiful friend!

Chris and Paris, my biggest surprise heartbeats. There's no better way I could have ended this book than with the start of your lives. Of all the different kinds of love I've known, the kind I have for you is my favorite! I hope you grow up reading libraries full of books with me, just give it sleep, espresso and time!